BRIDGING OVER
with
GUIDANCE

More Books by
Nancy Wiltgen

In the Garden

BRIDGING OVER
with
GUIDANCE

My Personal Relationship with God

NANCY WILTGEN

iUniverse, Inc.
Bloomington

Bridging Over With Guidance
My Personal Relationship with God

iUniverse books may be ordered through booksellers or by contacting:

iUniverse
1663 Liberty Drive
Bloomington, IN 47403
www.iuniverse.com
1-800-Authors (1-800-288-4677)

ISBN: 978-1-4759-0545-8 (sc)
ISBN: 978-1-4759-0543-4 (hc)
ISBN: 978-1-4759-0544-1 (ebk)

Library of Congress Control Number: 2012905565

Printed in the United States of America

iUniverse rev. date: 04/21/2012

CONTENTS

Introduction xi

Bridging Over with Guidance 1

Many are Called 3

Spiritual Battles 7

You are the Student 10

A New Concept... 17

Spiritual Director 20

The Gift of Visions.. 35

Spiritual Warfare 44

Linking and Speaking in Tongues... 50

Weapons of Warfare 55

Harvest of Souls 63

Walk with Me 71

ABOUT THE AUTHOR

In 1994 I had an encounter with God, and it changed my life. There was no choice on my part as I entered into a new spiritual realm; I began to have visions of the Blessed Mother, and she gave me direction on this new path in my life. I didn't realize at the time that I was also battling Satan, who was out to destroy my life.

I was led to read my Bible, and I began to see and understand how the spiritual world and the real world were being blended together. After a period of time, the visions of Mary were taken away. I learned I had pedestals and barriers that needed to be broken in order for me to grow spiritually, and I also learned about spiritual warfare and revivals. Yes, with the help of the Holy Spirit, I was bridging over to the new spiritual realm with guidance. Thank God I made it!

In loving memory of "Little Monk":
Rev. Redemptus J. Short, OCD
November 26, 1917-November 13, 2010

DEDICATION

I would like to thank the Lord for all the words written in this book without our conversations it wouldn't have been possible. You are so amazing!

I would like to dedicate this book to someone very special in my life. Without her; I may not have reached out in prayer for help. Because of prayer my life changed drastically for the better. A whole new way of life was opened to me through the Holy Spirit and with guidance from the Holy Spirit; I have been able to touch many lives around me. In turn, their lives also changed as they reached out for God. The Lord refers to this as the linking process. My daughter linked to me during her time of stress and pain. It became an open door to my spiritual life. Thank you, Wendy.

Love you,
Mom

INTRODUCTION

Many years ago, in 1994, I began to have a personal relationship with the Lord. I did not know at the time that I was on a spiritual journey. In fact, I did not even know what a spiritual journey was.

It's true that as a child, I prayed all the time. I grew up Catholic, which gave me a very strong foundation in daily prayer. However, it was always a one-way conversation: I prayed and God listened. My biggest problem was that I never read the Bible.

Once I began to read the Bible, I learned that it is possible to have a conversation with our Lord through the Holy Spirit. I also learned that the devil can speak to us in many ways, for he likes to imitate the light of Christ and tries to take us down the wrong path.

As my faith grew like a small mustard seed, I became very strong mentally, and I could see the presence of God everywhere I looked. I learned that my relationship with the Blessed Mother was the key factor in my life that opened the door to my relationship with Jesus, which in turn led me to a path by which I would follow Jesus through the Holy Spirit. As Mary stepped back, my relationship with Jesus grew stronger and stronger all the time. I was led to read the Bible every day, which taught me many things about my life here on earth. I also learned that I have been battling Satan all my life; I just did not recognize his attacks. He hides himself very well, but through my relationship with the Holy Spirit, Satan's presence was revealed to me, and I was given the direction that I needed to live a peaceful life.

I said, "Yes, Lord, I am yours. Yes, I will continue to battle Satan, but now I know God will carry me through any problems that arise."

If you have problems, you can learn to recognize that Satan has you on a roller coaster and that he is after you. This is why your relationship with the Lord is so important; you can learn to listen for directions from the Holy Spirit and make a choice before entering the battle against evil. The Lord will give you the help you have been seeking.

It is your choice always, but the Lord is waiting for you to invite him into your life. There will be a judgment day, and you will be accountable for your actions. So listen for the voice of God. With his directions, you could help save a soul for God's kingdom and from hell.

It is my prayer that this journal will strengthen you on your spiritual journey with the Lord. I would like you to share in the close relationship that I have with our Lord and Savior; I pray that you will invite him into your life, ask for forgiveness for your past sins, and grow into a new level with Christ. With God's help, you, too, can bridge your real world with your spiritual world and blend them together as one.

BRIDGING OVER WITH GUIDANCE

Many years ago, I was just an ordinary person. I grew up with problems just like everyone else. Its true life has its share of problems. Does anyone know why these things happen to us? Of course, no one sits around thinking about why things happen to you in your daily life. Things just happen! The people you meet sometimes can steer you in the wrong direction or even pull you into their problems and without thinking, you can be involved in a whole new set of problems.

We are very fortunate if we have friends that last a lifetime and there are a few. Others just seem to fade in and out of our lives. Did you ever wonder why? Of course not.

Sometimes life takes a sudden change. This could be a move to a new area or perhaps a new job. It could even be the death of a loved one.

Most people are so busy with their plans for their daily lives that there is no time to sit and ponder or I should say, 'think' about why you are here and if there is a purpose for your existence. These questions sound silly, don't you think? Generation after generation, we walk in each other's footsteps never questioning the reason why, or perhaps afraid of disappointing others.

Sometimes strange things or events take place but we are afraid to share them with others for fear that we will be judged by them. Therefore, you quietly sit by and say nothing, or you have a choice in the matter. This is a chance to step out of the box and reach out to whatever is beyond your imagination. There you can find the purpose to why you are here, why there are problems, and who can help you by giving directions if you need help and are willing to listen and be obedient. It is not an easy lifestyle at the beginning and it is not for wimps! It takes courage and guts to stand up and fight for what you believe in. In the end, you will find out that it was worth the battle you were fighting for, for yourself and others around you.

Doors were opened to me that I did not know existed. I fell into a whole new world. There was a silent passageway that connected me to this new world and it was not by my choice. I did not understand what was happening, but I knew God would carry me through anything. In a case of perfect timing, God guided a friend of mine, who handed me a poem entitled "Guidance":

My eyes drew back to the word *Guidance*.
When I saw *G*: I thought of *God*, followed by *u* and *i*.
"*God, u* and *i dance*."
God, you and I dance.
As I lowered my head, I became willing to trust
that I would get guidance about my life.

I would like to share my story with you on how it all began.

MANY ARE CALLED

February 2008

PRAYER:

Dear Lord;

Why are these things happening to me? I do not understand. There were pictures in my mind and they were in color and they moved freely about as I watched them. It seemed as if I were looking into another dimension. I was hearing and seeing the Blessed Virgin Mary. Lord was I having a mental breakdown?

ANSWER:

My Nancy;

You were called to a wonderful new and exciting life style for a reason. Before you were born, I knew that you would choose me. Even when you were a little girl unknowingly, you had a relationship with me through my mother, Mary. Through a child's eyes, you were searching for me, your savior. As an adult, there were many things you needed to learn about the Holy Spirit. Many barriers needed to be broken. As a new creation in Christ, I was able to touch many lives through you. You are a new springtime to others of sharing our stories and praying for lost souls. You are a strong warrior that will lead others to have a relationship with me. Doors will open in my timing. Many are called and few are chosen, my little dancer.

Savior—means a person who rescues someone or something from disastrous circumstance.

⌒✺⌒

April 20, 2008

PRAYER:

My Lord;

Is there a purpose for me going through a time of having visions and hearing voices speaking to me?

ANSWER:

Yes, my child;

At the beginning of your journey with Me you did not understand what was happening to you for a reason.

The visions of Mary allowed you to find comfort and peace with her. Under my directions, she led you to me, your Savior. When Mary spoke audibly to you it was an opening for a rebirth for you into the spiritual realm and at the same time the other voices you were hearing was that of Satan pulling you into another direction. I was there with you all the time my child.

⌒✺⌒

April 27, 2008

PRAYER:

Did my spiritual journey start because I was praying to you about my daughter's problems? I remember all of a sudden I felt as if I was standing right next to you and I began to speak to you as if you were another human being. I had never done that before . . . was that wrong?

ANSWER:

No, my child;

Your spiritual journey started with prayer because you no longer felt in control of the situation. Prayer is a conversation with God that many people do not understand. For many years you recited prayers from memory, it was a one-way conversation. You were never taught how to sit and listen for the still voice of God, but I heard every prayer you said from a small child until now. Through conversations, I am able to direct your path. Do you remember when you fully understood it was me you were speaking to, that you began to ask forgiveness for the things you had done wrong in your past. This is what is called repentance. Many people do not fully understand the word repentance, but through prayers the door was opened to you to begin this new life with me, Your Savior.

Conversation-an informal spoken exchange of thoughts and feelings
Repentance-remorse (sorry) for past conduct (behavior)

May 4, 2008

PRAYER:

My Dear Lord;

When the visions began and I was hearing voices speaking to me I felt so confused, yet the voice of Mary told me where to go and who to talk to. Many were people I did not know very well and some were strangers. Yet they were full of information I needed at that time. I felt I was walking blindly into a situation. I did not understand. Because I was so confused I never even put it together that it was a religious experience. When I finally realized it was you, Lord, that was speaking to me, I felt unworthy that you would want to spend time talking to me and I need to know if this is possible? I thought this only happened to people in the Bible and saints. These are the important people of when you came to earth, and walked among them, people in bible stories.

ANSWER:

My child;

Many people at some time in their lives experience a vision or hear a voice call to them but dismiss this event as something strange or a special event that happened in their lives. With many, it only occurs once or twice in their lifetime. They do not put it together that it was a gift from God; linking the real world with the spiritual side. Many people hear about it but never experience the spiritual side so they do not fully understand what is involved in a calling from God.

My child, you were walking in blind faith and seeking me as you never did before. I placed all the right people in the right timing to guide you closer to me, your Lord and Savior. As for feeling unworthy many people who are called to do God's work feel this way. Many people question, "Why me?" However, I know the outcome and purpose for each individual. You are my vessels that can be used to touch many lives around you. You are my hands and my feet. The Bible is full of stories of people on a spiritual journey. Each has a special story to tell with meanings to teach others about their walk with God. With Mary, she said, "let your will be done to me." With Jonah he ran. With many, the touch of God changed their entire life and gave them a full purpose for serving God. My child you are my hope to touch many people's lives. I have given you a strong foundation in your spiritual journey with me. I am a God for all generations, my child.

Spiritual Battles

Prayer:

Dear Lord;

I want to thank you for the beautiful visions of Mary that I saw in my mind's eye. I felt so close to her even giving her a kiss on the cheek mentally. But I don't understand why did you stop the visions of Mary coming to me? I felt that I slipped into a state of depression for nearly six weeks after the vision of Mary stopped. Why?

Answer:

My dear child;

I sent Mary to you for a very special reason. Because I knew you had a strong bond with her since your childhood. As I watched you stand on a kneeler and talked to her as if she was alive. But it was only a statue, do you remember sitting in the front pew and staring at the statue of Mary while you watched for the lips to move but they never did? The nuns told you that Mary would speak to you some day but it was in my timing that this occurred. Mary was my gateway to Me. You needed to break away from the real world and come follow Me, your Lord and Savior. It was during this time that you learned that not all visions come from God. Do you remember the time Mary came to you and you wondered why the veil was over her face? Then the veil fell open revealing the face of a space creature. That vision was not of God. I know how you tried to block the

7

visions that were coming to your mind. It was something you needed to learn. As for the depression, you were struggling between the real world and the spiritual world at the same time. Mary was your comfort zone in both worlds. She was the link between both worlds. So, my child during this time you had to learn to move forward with my help. It was a time of learning about spiritual battles and still be able to walk in the real world with my help, your Lord and Savior, my child.

c##

May 18, 2008

PRAYER:

My Dear Lord;

Before this all began, I do not remember hearing the phrase "spiritual battles." I feel as if some sort of veil was lifted before my eyes. I was looking into a whole new world unknown to me. Is this coming from my imagination Jesus?

ANSWER:

No my child;

This is not your imagination. It is I, Jesus Christ of Nazareth the Nazarene that speaks to you my child. It is I that seeks a personal relationship with every human being. Through the love of Christ, I can direct the path of each person. Yes, my child the veil was lifted from your eyes so that you might learn about the attacks of Satan. This is all known as spiritual battles.

You were not aware of the ways of Satan at the beginning of your spiritual journey. Satan was out to destroy you in many ways. Do you remember the time when you were told, through your thoughts, that if you drove your car through a wall and you died that all the voices you were hearing would stop?

There were many things that happened to you during this time in your mind and in your real world. Satan wanted you to think you were going crazy. But I interceded to help you fight through the battles. That is why I gave you a spiritual director, Sister Elizabeth, who prayed for you and your husband; I also gave you a spiritual family, of which some of them also heard me, your Lord and Savior. This was the beginning of your strong foundation in Christ. You were strong links with each other to help fight Satan's attacks. In your minds and the real world, my presence is always with you my child.

YOU ARE THE STUDENT

May 25, 2008

PRAYER:

My Dear Lord;

At the beginning of my spiritual journey, I felt like I was attending a school in my mind. You were the teacher and there were no books from which to learn. Were you combining the two worlds together and why did this take place?

ANSWER:

My child;

You had moved into a new level in Christ. It was I, Jesus Christ of Nazareth that was teaching you to keep your focus on me. While you were walking in both worlds at the same time, it was I that began to teach you about colors. When you see the color green, it was to remind you that the Garden of Eden was a luscious green when it was first created. Blue was the color of Mary's dress. Yellow stood for the Son of God. Red was for the blood of Christ. Purple stood for royalty.

I also taught you about numbers. Each number represented a meaning. The number one stood for "One God." Two was to remind you that there were two worlds going on at the same time. Three represents the Father, the Son and the Holy Spirit. Five, there are five decades to a rosary. Whenever you see a set of fives, it signals a high five between you and I.

Between the colors and numbers, it kept your mind busy and you focus on the things I was teaching you in the real world. I was blending in the stories from the Bible. For many years, Satan had consumed your thought patterns. Now as a child of God, you had to learn a new way of thinking, and be able to listen and follow me, your Lord and Savior. I needed you as a vessel to touch other lives around you. You are my ambassador to reach others and teach them how God has touched your life. You will connect with others in my timing so that other people will learn to be open to the Holy Spirit in their lives. You will also be human links with one another as a support group to fight Satan. I know it has been difficult for you at times living this lifestyle, but many people who follow Christ have to give up many things for the love of Christ, my child.

June 1, 2008

PRAYER:

My Dear Lord;

This is true. My thoughts were very negative before this happened to me. I can look back now and see how my mind seemed to be on a treadmill, with thoughts being played over and over. I took it for granted that this was normal. I did not realize that this was not how others think. I can see now how you broke my patterns of thinking.

When I began to change, I felt as if I fell into an underground world. Yet I met other people who understood what was happening to me. Lord, do you remember at the beginning of my spiritual journey you gave me three songs that blended both of my worlds together. Was there a special reason why this happened?

ANSWER:

Yes my child;

I gave you three songs that blended your real world with your spiritual side. Each song had words, which were a message to you from Me, your Lord and Savior. The first song I gave you was *Let It Be*. The main message was when mother Mary comes to me speaking works of wisdom "let it be."

The next song I gave you was *In the Garden*. The words I chose for you were "and He walks with me and He talks with me, and He tells me I am His own."

The final song I gave you was *One Day at a Time*. The words that reflect your journey were: "Show me the stairway I have to climb, Lord for my sake, teach me to take one day at a time." This is what I call puzzle pieces. As time went on, I gave you more pieces to build on. Your love for me needed to be blended into your real world. I wanted to show you that the Bible stories could come to life, your life my child.

June 8, 2008

PRAYER:

Dear Lord;

Can you please tell me how the Bible stories are connected with my real life? At the beginning of my spiritual journey, I was told that I was pioneering in my field. Lord, what does this mean?

ANSWER:

My child;

Many people grow up and never read the Bible. Some never attend a church service. Yet it is I that probes the mind and tests your heart. I chose people not because of their ability but I chose the ones who are open to the Holy Spirit. These are my vessels who become leaders in my name. They are my chosen people. Through your writings, I will reveal to you and others the presence of God was with you all your life.

There is a Bible verse that says, "Be still and know that I am God." Many people never take the time to listen for the voice of God, but I have spoken to you many times audibly and sometimes as a whisper from nowhere, but most of the times through your thoughts. People do not realize that all their thoughts are not theirs for Satan also speaks to you. This is called temptation. But through the renewal of our minds, we can learn to discern what God is teaching us and who is speaking to us. My child I know how difficult this was for you at the time but as time passed you were able to teach your spiritual family members how to discern their thought patterns so they were able to walk with God and make the right decisions. There are many lazy Christians who do not want to listen or are not willing to do what is asked of them. When this happens the linking with another person is broken and puzzle pieces are missing. My work can't be accomplished. Many people are not aware of the presence of God in their lives, but I have taught you how to look for signs and wonders as you became aware of your path with me. At the beginning of your journey, you reluctantly reached out to five of our closest friends, Nancy, Shirley, JoAnn, Patty and Cathy. These women were your strength with the real world. They gave you words of encouragement. All of you are women of strong faith in God. However, not all paths follow the same direction, for there was one who was following the Lord but not at the same level as you. As a pioneer, you were openly speaking about how God was working in your life, teaching the examples I taught you from the beginning of your spiritual journey, my child.

June 8, 2008

PRAYER:

My Lord;

You have taught me that there is a difference between being religious and having a relationship with God. Is this true?

ANSWER:

Yes my child;

There is a big difference between being religious and having a relationship with me, your Lord and Savior. Do you remember when you were little how you went to Catholic Mass everyday of the week?

REPLY:

"Yes, Lord I remember", I said.

ANSWER:

Do you remember going to First Holy Communion in your white dress and veil?

REPLY:

"Yes, Lord I remember!"

ANSWER:

When you were confirmed?

REPLY:

"Yes, Lord I remember."

ANSWER:

My child you were baptized with water the day you were born in the hospital because they thought you were going to die but on February 23rd with your grandparents you were once again baptized with water at the church. You were already on a spiritual journey then but did not know it yet. True?

REPLY:

"Yes my Lord", I said.

ANSWER:

My child that is a religious journey. I watched you pray your rosaries all the time and many times in tears as you groped for me, looking for answers. Statues, candles, and churches were an important part of your life. This was tradition for you my child, but when I called to you, you were once again baptized, but this time with the Holy Spirit. You had the renewing of the mind and were taught over again how to walk in the spirit, which is not easy. You were strong because of the way you were brought up religiously. Satan did not want you to succeed. So you were taught by revelation from Me your Lord and Savior that this was something you knew nothing about. My child, I do not dwell in sanctuaries made by man, for I live within each of you, and you needed to learn this, I laugh to myself when you tell others now I give more money to the poor.

Now I tithe every Sunday. I pray more now than I ever did in my life. I attend more church services and stay for hours and it does not bother me at all, because I can feel the presence of God.

This is the life of walking with God in the guidance of the Holy Spirit my child.

A New Concept

June 19, 2008

Prayer:

My Dear Lord;

Earlier you spoke of the word levels. What does the word level mean to you? I have found that many people get upset or feel offended when that word is used. This is a new word for me and it is confusing in the real world.

Answer:

My child;

The word level can be used in many ways. Most people think of a rank on a scale. True?

Reply:

"Yes, Lord."

Answer:

Many Christians want to compare themselves with other Christians. They want to feel superior to others. Some people just do not realize that walking with God has a completely different meaning in the spiritual realm. Each person deals with different situations in their lives. As I teach you how to deal with real world problems, you are given a choice to follow me. As you grow and become closer to me your Lord and Savior, you grow to a new level of understanding in Christ Jesus.

As you learn to deal with problems of forgiveness and many other things, you master at that time a solution for a problem and as you grow, you move to another level of understanding in my eyes. Many people are put to the test everyday to demonstrate the level of understanding I have taught you. Through the Bible, pastors, evangelists, teachers and yes, taking the time to sit and listen to Me. As I guide each of you through your daily problems. For I am with you always my child.

June 20, 2008

PRAYER:

My Dear Lord;

It is difficult trusting a life style that is unknown to me, hearing a voice speaking but seeing no one around me. I remember when Sister Elizabeth was my spiritual director, she once told me that I was walking in two worlds, and I needed to pull one foot over to the other side. I remember crying for weeks and asking her how do I do this. She said she did not know how, and she said I know you are pulling a lot of people with you. Then all of a sudden, it happened and there I was walking with you Lord. Do you remember?

ANSWER:

Yes, my child;

You were struggling because there was no one to help you. Again the word level applies to this situation, you were learning how to listen to my voice and I was teaching you that Satan can also speak. I was teaching you the word 'discernment'. You were learning to pick apart your thoughts. I was teaching you that Satan can imitate the Light of Christ, Jesus.

My child, do you remember how I taught you to ask who speaks to me? I would reply, "It is I, Jesus Christ of Nazareth, the Nazarene." Sometimes you heard Satan. You were very fearful of that response. But it was I who taught you to mentally say, "I rebuke you in the name of Jesus Christ. I pour the precious blood of Jesus over me." Then the inner voice was quiet.

Many people hear voices speaking to them but have never been taught how to discern because it is a subject that no one speaks of in the real world. Like you, many people hear voices but do not realize that they are having a spiritual connection with God. Especially if they do not read the Bible, attend church or read books on the topic of the Holy Spirit. Yes, my child you did step from one world into another by fully listening to the voices you were hearing as I guided you in faith. It was then I began to blend the two worlds together. Others are not fully open to listening and learning because they do not realize what is happening to them. Because of your religious upbringing, you clung to "Mary the Mother of Peace" who guided your footsteps to me, your Lord and Savior. It was my Mother through her voice and visions that guided you back to Holy Hill, where you met the Carmelite monks. One in particular I chose for you to meet was Father Short. I told you to call him "Little Monk." He is a very special man and very close to me. The next day you met another man who was a fundraiser for the Cathedral at that time. He was a worldlier priest, but I chose him to let you know that you were a Catholic charismatic person. It was the opening to a new whole world that was being exposed to you. Many people did not even know that this existed in the Catholic Church. But my child, I wanted you to teach others about this new life style you were learning about. That is why I connected you to Sister Elizabeth as your mentor. As you later learned, she was a teacher of spiritual direction at Kino College. Through you, a door was opened to her. You were linking with one another through me, your Lord and Savior, my child.

Spiritual Director

June 20, 2008

Prayer:

My Dear Lord;

What exactly is a spiritual director? At the beginning of my spiritual journey, I did not even know what direction to turn to for help. The voice of Mary your mother led me to my parish priest but he could not help me either. He laughed at me and wanted to know why I thought Mary would speak to me when he had traveled around the world looking for a connection with God and could not find it. His words were "you are only a white woman." I was so deeply hurt by his comments and also the fact that the priest did not believe what I was telling him was indeed true.

Answer:

My child;

A spiritual director or mentor is someone who is close to God in their daily lives. It can be a man or woman. That is why I picked out Sister Elizabeth for you. Do you remember how you found her?

"Yes, Lord through a Catholic paper. I found the name of a priest and behind his name it said spiritual director."

Yes, my child but remember when you called you were told that he was having health problems and was not able to meet with you. But the secretary told you that she knew someone who could help you. I closed the door to the priest but open it for Sister Elizabeth. My child at the beginning of your spiritual journey the voice of my mother led you to your family priest. I was trying to teach you that not all priests or pastors hear God. Some also are at different levels of understanding God. When you were led by the voice of Mary to go and speak to the priest, I was giving him the opportunity to work and pray with you. However, that did not happen. I was also teaching you that the devil can use anyone as an open vessel to hurt you so that you will not continue on with your spiritual journey. I am sorry you were hurt by his words but when someone is on a path with me your Lord and Savior race has no boundaries. You my child, I have chosen you to walk among the Mexican people for a reason. Since you were a small child, I knew that you were not prejudice in any way. I know that you have a caring and loving soul my child.

June 25, 2008

PRAYER:

My Dear Lord;

Over the years, I have learned so many things that I was not aware of before my spiritual journey. I am still puzzled as to why I had so many problems in the prayer groups I attended.

ANSWER:

My child;

You were looking for answers from other people. First, you had to learn that answers come from me your Lord and Savior. Do you remember the first prayer group you went to looking for help?

REPLY:

"Yes, Lord."

ANSWER:

Instead, you were treated like a child. I remember how frustrated you felt. At the start of the prayer session, you were told to hold your books and sing and do you remember what I told you to do?

REPLY:

"Yes Lord, you told me to raise my hands. But Lord a woman came over to me and told me I had to hold my book. She lifted my book and put in into my hands. I felt embarrassed by this Lord."

ANSWER:

My child;

I know but the next week when you went back, you were running late, and they ran out of books and again I said lift your holy hands. This time nothing happened to you. My child the reason why people lift their hands while singing and praying is because it is an outward sign of surrender to the Living God. You were there to teach this group that it was acceptable in My eyes and this came from the Bible my child.

PRAYER:

My Dear Lord;

As time went by you led me to another prayer group. However, things did not get any better there. Lord, I was amazed at how the people would sit and give a message from God. This was all new to me. I had never observed this before. Was there a special reason why you sent me there?

ANSWER:

Yes, my child;

I was teaching you about the gift of prophesy which is "a message from God," to the group. Do you remember how you would sit and listen, as the people would speak a message?

REPLY:

"Yes Lord."

ANSWER:

Do you remember how I had interrupted your line of thinking and told you, "Nancy, this is prophesy." I would speak to you and you would repeat what I was telling you.

REPLY:

"Yes Lord, but Lord; do you remember how the ladies would take me to the back room after the meetings. There I was told that I was out of order and the prophesy was given at the wrong time. Then they would pray over me. I did not understand what was happening. I would leave the meetings in tears. But each week you asked me to go back. I was trying to be obedient to you, but each time it was repeated."

ANSWER:

My child do you remember the man named Edward who was a leader of another prayer group who attended the meetings with you and your husband?

REPLY:

"Yes Lord."

ANSWER:

I was using him to teach this group that the Lord is in charge of the meetings and not the core members.

My child, you were given the gift of prophesy with Edward for a long time. It was I who took this gift away from the core because of their behavior. Sometimes people do not remember that the Holy Spirit is in charge. I was trying to show them that I needed to be included in the meetings my child.

PRAYER:

My Dear Lord;

Every week I cried because I did not want to go back to the meetings because I felt so humiliated. I could not understand why I needed to return each week. The reason I returned was you asked me to.

ANSWER:

My child;

You were an open vessel for the people who were attending the meetings. Do you remember the elderly lady who attended the meetings?

Reply:

"Yes Lord."

Answer:

Do you remember how your Bibles were mixed up? Do you remember the woman with the long hair who sought you out for private prayer at your home? Do you remember the outspoken woman you met there? This all took time for you to come together and become friends. I put you together as a second spiritual family. This took time to assemble you as a group. I used Edward to help guide you through this storm in your life, my child.

cll

June 30, 2008

Prayer:

My Dear Lord;

Are people at different levels in prayer groups?

Answer:

Yes, my child;

It is just like the growing process in your real life. First, you are held in your mother's arms. Then you learn to crawl. Then you begin to stand but not steady as you hang on to the furniture. Then at some point in time, you let go but you walk only a few steps. Then as time goes by you become steadier and move with more confidence and eventually you begin to run. You see my child the different levels?

Reply:

"Yes Lord."

Answer:

Just like in your spiritual growth, the same process takes place. Just as a child stumbles and falls but gets up, resumes walking so does the spiritual life continues on only in the spiritual journey the devil doesn't want you to have a relationship with Me, your Lord and Savior, so attacks come against you to discourage you from walking with Me. It takes a strong individual and will power to walk with Me. As in prayer groups many people who are leaders forget about the new comers who are not familiar or are just learning about their spiritual journey are over looked. Many expect you to know everything they do. That is why it was so difficult for you, my child.

July 1, 2008

Prayer:

My Dear Lord;

So many things happened to me at the prayer groups. Was there a reason why I did not fit in?

Answer:

Yes, my child;

There are many reasons why this happened. First, you did not belong to their inner circle of friends, so it made it more difficult for you to discern. Many times the flesh or personal preference interferes with decision-making and not all answers are from God. Second, you were hearing the Lord speak to you more often than the others, and they knew this for I gave them confirmation that this was happening. You were at a different level than they were, but for a reason, my reasons, my child. Third, you were sent there to teach them to be more open to the Holy Spirit. Sometimes they understood and sometimes not, and some were afraid that you were there to take over the leadership, but that was not the case. Fourth, some felt threatened by you because sometimes you were rested in the spirit by Me, your Lord and Savior. Some groups felt that only a few designated people are allowed to pray over others but this is not true my child.

July 2, 2008

PRAYER:

My Dear Lord;

Why is it that people who are Christians seem to be one way but act another? In the churches where you have taken me, I have found a split of people who are religious and some spiritual.

ANSWER:

My child;

Once again, there are different levels of Christians and religious people. Do you remember before you were spiritual the reason why you went to church? You went because you were taught if you did not go to church you would go to hell. Many people think this way. Some of the people are there to build up the Church by this. I mean the building and its contents, but they are missing the most important aspect of their lives. Just as the spiritually led people come to church because many are called by the Lord. They sing and praise God and have a relationship with Me, your Lord and Savior. The problem is what they learn from the pastor is not carried out in their everyday lives. Many put Me on a shelf until the next Sunday or people tend to drift in and out of their spiritual journeys when it accommodates their lifestyle. As for the people who are not born again, the same process takes place. The devil prowls the earth with every temptation trying to test people to sin, no matter how they are walking with God. For the ones that are not aware of the presence of God, temptations can destroy their lives and others around them, until they reach a point of destruction. Then people begin to search and cry out to Me, your Lord and Savior, my child.

July 3, 2008

PRAYER:

My Dear Lord;

Many people do not speak about spiritual journeys in their lives outside of the church settings. Yet after I began to hear you Lord, you brought people into my home and you told me to share with them that I was hearing you speak to me. I was so frightened Lord that I had made a mistake in doing this because after a few days they came back and some of them also began to hear you. Was this a mistake?

ANSWER:

No, my child;

Even though I brought people to your home to share your stories not all were given the gift of hearing me, your Lord and Savior. This group of people that was brought together formed your first spiritual family. You all bonded beautifully together. Each of you had a purpose to fill in your spiritual family. My child, I brought Jan and Earl into your life because at that time they desperately needed help financially and mainly because they needed God to help direct their lives. At first no one quite knew what was happening to you as a group, but these families of different religions was joined to you. Do you remember how the Methodist leadership came to their home to listen to the stories of what was happening to you and how the devil was attacking you and Earl. My child, they told all of you what was happening was that you were receiving the "Gifts of the Holy Spirit."

The attacks of Satan against all of you were because Satan did not want this to succeed. The young couple with the baby also needed God in their lives. Financially, they were struggling but I chose the woman to hear me because her family came from a Christian background. The other person I chose was a young woman who was attending college at that time. There were many reasons why I had chosen her. She also was from a Christian background. As a group of different denominations, I was trying to teach you that you are all my children. You were all created to have a relationship with me, your Lord and Savior, my child.

July 4, 2008

PRAYER:

My Dear Lord;

I had never heard of a spiritual family before I started hearing your voice. Why did you create something like this? Was there a special purpose for having this group together?

ANSWER:

Yes my child;

In the Bible when I walked the earth, my apostles and some women were my spiritual family. They gave up families and personal possessions to come follow Me. Through my examples, I was teaching them to connect with my Heavenly Father through prayer and fasting. Yet my spiritual family was there to connect with me for everyday living, just as your spiritual family had a strong bond with one another. You were able to confirm things, talk about the visions you were given and mainly to openly speak about the things I was speaking to you individually. You were all learning at the same time, plus you were all learning about obedience. In this structure, you complimented each other through the different churches you attended. All of you had a strong relationship with my Mother Mary, although this was very puzzling to you my child. You had this presumption that Mary spoke only to Catholics, not true, my child. She became the link to me your Lord and Savior. Do you remember when you all reached a point in time where you all grew to the same spiritual level? Then I decided through a meeting with Sister Elizabeth that it was time to move on. What a blessing too many people they have become. Some of them have become leaders in their churches when they returned. They are my extensions of myself walking among the people. I know you were very depressed after the family broke away. Many of the daily phone calls were gone. Caring for the two little girls and mainly exchanging or comparing notes on how I was speaking to you individually was gone. Just as in the real world, children leave and move on, so it was with your spiritual family. It was a season of time. It was a growing time for each of you my child.

July 5, 2008

PRAYER:

My Dear Lord;

It was very difficult at first moving from a spiritual family into the real world. I did not really know who I could trust. Do you remember Lord the problems I had with my closest friends?

ANSWER:

Yes, my child;

At the beginning of your spiritual journey, you were learning how to trust in the voice of God. I know it was very difficult for you at the beginning. I watched you reach out to people whom you had known for many years. Do you remember the woman who was your closest friend but when you told her what was happening to you she rejected you as her friend, because she was embarrassed by your behavior. Also she did not hear God. I was teaching you to reach out to the people who would understand, that is why I removed her from your life and into a different position in the factory. At that time, a new woman became your leader, a Hispanic lady. Do you remember when you were told mentally to tell her about hearing Mary and seeing visions, but you were afraid to share this information because of the loss of your friendship with the other woman and you feared for the loss of your job. After a few weeks, you told her and your life began to change. I put the two of you together for a very special reason. This woman has a strong love for Christ. She was open to the Holy Spirit. In the years to come she and her family became an important part of your spiritual journey. Many times I watched as you prayed together in the factory, in your home, in the hospitals and churches. It has touched my heart to see the closeness the two of you have had over the years. You had also given her family strength when needed. As time passed by you had learned to obey me your Lord and Savoir as I began to link you to others so that you could pray with these people and help them get through stressful situations. Many people could feel the presence of the Holy Spirit when you were near or touched them. Many of these people were of Hispanic origin. In addition, do you remember the young Hispanic girl who needed help with groceries and the purchase of three green cards through the Catholic Social Services? How strange that their names were Angel, Moses and Mama. Through you, I was giving them the opportunity to start a new life. The reason why I took your old friends away was because I needed you to step out in faith and help Me save the ones that were praying for answers from God, my child.

July 5, 2008

PRAYER:

My Dear Lord;

I was never aware that there were so many hurting people around me. As you began to guide me, I had to learn how to listen to your voice. It was difficult at times because Satan also speaks to us. I wonder Lord are people aware of the thought patterns that run through their minds?

ANSWER:

No, my child;

People are not aware of the negative thoughts that run through their minds. Many times, I speak to people but their minds are like roller coasters. In the Bible, it says, "be still and know that I am God." Many people do not take the time to sit and read their Bibles, listen to Christian music or even take time to pray. People feel that they cannot even have a conversation or prayer time with me your Lord and Savior just because it's daytime. Many are taught that you should only pray at night, yet I am with you all the time. I see all the events that take place in your life, good and bad. Prayer is a very significant part of your life and yet this is over looked, even by Christian people. It is important to stay in tuned with me for guidance in your everyday life. I am able to guide you through scenarios that could have had a bad ending, but if you pray and listen I can guide you through a very peaceful journey. Many times as I speak to people, they do not want to listen to me because it is difficult to follow the path with Christ. Sometimes we have to give up personal property like our money, clothes, and yes, especially our time. The outcome is overwhelming and it has to be a personal choice on your part. Satan also speaks through your thoughts. My child do you remember the time when your thoughts told you that if you drove your car through a wall that all the voices you were hearing would stop? Yes, Satan was out to destroy your life. Just as an alcoholic hears one more drink will not hurt, and an addict hears that they can shoot up only if they want to. A smoker thinks he is in control, but these are addictions that Satan feeds your minds. Some people hear to kill their children. This is not so. The Bible states "do not kill." Even the unborn child suffers because of Satan's attack in the mind my child.

⌒ん⌒

July 12, 2008

PRAYER:

My Dear Lord;

There are many different views on how the mind works. Yet I cannot even explain to others how fascinating it is to sit and listen to you Lord. Many people write about hearing God and how to find you, but that was not the case with me. They say it is a process of learning to find you. Is this true?

ANSWER:

My child;

Some people attend churches, read books and many meditate. They are searching for me your Lord and Savior. But it is I that finds each person at a particular time in their life. Not all people hear God audibly as you do my child. Your experiences with me are somewhat different. There are times when you hear me as speaking on a phone with someone and most of the time it is by your thought process of speaking to me as I answer you with thoughts. I am able to dismiss your thoughts and bring others to your mind. People just are not fully aware of this happening to themselves. They do not put it together that this is a gift from God. Many scientists, musicians, writers and preachers only to name a few are highly gifted people. All the work they produce comes from their thoughts. The brain is a very important and unique part of the body. With this brain comes the choice on how we wish to use the information that is developed in this process.

I, your creator, can show you many things but it is through personal choice if it is carried out; some thoughts are not of God and thoughts like these are used for destruction for yourself or others. Each person is given a path to follow. It is their choice, life or death circumstance take place all the time in one's life. Peace or depression takes place during this time. People do not recognize that a simple choice they make can touch others around them in many ways.

As couples fight, it can touch the lives of their children to a point of destruction for them. Families can fall apart yet man does not see how Satan's underlying works can destroy several lives at a time. People need to learn the attacks of Satan through the thought process. There are many people who do not take the time to learn or just wish not to make a choice to better themselves. Some are not even aware that there is a choice to be made. They take it for granted when I give them gifts in their lives. They never recognize that it is coming from me. They miss out on a life that could connect them with me, your Lord and Savior. They are my missing links that could touch another person's life when needed. Many people suffer because of this. People feel inadequate with the idea that they could talk with me, but the Bible is full of stories of men and women who had lives just like now full of problems. These people receive visions, heard Gods voice and spoke in other tongues. All these things still take place in people's lives my child.

THE GIFT OF VISIONS

July 12, 2008

PRAYER:

My Dear Lord;

You spoke of visions; do people understand what this really means?

ANSWER:

No, my child;

In your real world, people do not comprehend what a vision is unless they experience it themselves. When you began your spiritual journey, I gave you a picture in your mind of a woman dressed in blue and white. You heard her voice speak audibly to you. I allowed you to see this vision move freely in your mind as she approached you from a distance as she moved closer to you. This vision was one of my mother, Mary. I allowed this because of your connection with her since your childhood. I knew you would be accepting of this vision. Many people receive visions in your real world. They are called visionaries.

The approach of my mother Mary was the opening of a door that led you to me your Lord and Savior. In addition, it was an obstacle that needed to be broken. It allowed you to move freely to me your Lord and Savior. As your journey moved forward, you realized that most of your prayer life was with her and not me.

As you continued on your journey with me, I led you to many women who had the name of Mary or some form of that name. It became a trail of reminders of how you entered your walk with me. Your reverence and love for my worldly mother had touched my heart. Not all people on spiritual journeys receive visions. It is important to remember that not all visions come from God.

My child, do you remember the time you had a vision of my mother coming towards you and you wondered why the veil was covering her face?

REPLY:

"Yes Lord."

ANSWER:

But as she approached you the veil fell open revealing the face of a space creature you had seen in a movie years ago when you were a teenager.

I remember how you tried to mentally block the visions coming to you at that time. I was trying to teach you that not all visions come from me your Lord and Savior. I saw how mentally tired you became from doing this, but time passed and your visions returned. I was teaching you through this process. Do you remember the man whom I told you to tell him about the visions you were seeing? I brought to his mind how to relieve the stress that came with that vision. It was a story about a cookbook entitled, *"How to Serve Man"*, but this man told you to take the cookbook and mentally turn it over and look at what you see. I remember you crying for hours after that for the vision I sent you was a picture of myself hanging on the cross. *"How to Serve Man,"* my child.

July 12, 2008

PRAYER:

My Dear Lord;

I want to thank you for that special vision you gave me of you hanging on the cross. It stopped the devil from tormenting me through my mind. For I was thinking this was all coming from outer space and something had taken over my body and mind.

ANSWER:

No, my child;

The devil wanted you to think this way, because it would interfere with your walk with me. My child, do you remember the other visions I gave you?

One morning as you were showering, you looked up and saw me as I was standing there watching you. You quickly tried to cover yourself but as you looked again, I was turned around and you saw me from the back but I was holding a dental mirror. I spoke and said it is fog resistant because you love hot showers. I remember how you broke out laughing. I was teaching you that I see you at all times. Even in your nakedness.

Then there was the time you were working at the press in the factory when all of a sudden in your minds eye you saw a beautiful picture of a daisy. I remember the big smile you gave me and mentally said thank you Lord. Within seconds, all the petals of the flower fell off except for one. I saw the disappointed look on your face and the smile was gone. You mentally said "Oh, my flower." I gave you a closer look at the petal. You then saw a magnifying glass being held over the one petal. I saw you mentally looking through it and again your smile returned as you read "I love u", and you mentally responded "I love you, too Lord." Then you mentally asked, "Why the magnifying glass?" I responded, "You have bad eyes." I was showing you I know your every need.

Another time I gave you a vision of me, from the back side, where I was sitting at an old fashioned desk. It was surrounded with lots of candles and in my hand was a feather quill and I was writing in an old book.

You were fascinated as you were watching me. You mentally came closer and looked over my shoulder to see what I was writing, but the pages were blank. I heard you mentally say, "They are blank!" I responded, "invisible ink." I remember how you began to laugh. I was teaching you that I have a sense of humor my child.

⌒ℳ⌒

July 14, 2008

PRAYER:

My Dear Lord;

I never realized that each vision represented something you were teaching me. Lord, do you remember the vision that took place in the church where I was raised?

ANSWER:

Yes, my child;

You went back to Holy Trinity Church searching for the statue of the pieta. It brought back memories to you of when you were a small girl. You used to stand on the kneeler and kiss the nail hole in the hand of the statue. When you arrived at the church with your husband, the priest had other plans so he gave you the keys to the church. I watched you as you looked through the church but the pieta had been moved, so you decided to leave because you could not find it. As you were exiting at the side door at the front of the alter you turned around and you thought you saw the statue. I watched you run down the aisle pushing your way through the double doors. You ran around the corner and there was your statue.

The vision I gave you was only the arm and hand, but you did not realize it until later. That vision was something very special and different from the other visions I had given you. For when you saw the statue you mentally took me out of the arms of my mother, you mentally took the crown of thorns and began to break them into pieces and you heard them cracking. Then you proceeded to pull them out. You were crying with pain in your heart. I gave you a vision of the white basin and a white towel. Then you mentally washed my body and wrapped it in a white sheet and held me just as the statue of the pieta, you were holding me. My child I was teaching you that you were connecting with me in a very special way. You no longer needed a statue to connect with me. You broke the crown of thorns and bathe me as a symbol of the past as how you saw me. Carrying me in the white sheet represented us as we walked into a new spiritual journey together. I am alive—the risen Christ, my child.

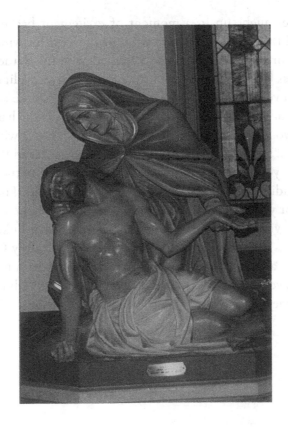

July 15, 2008

PRAYER:

My Dear Lord;

That particular vision was very precious moment for me. Why did I think I had seen the whole statue when I did not actually see it?

ANSWER:

My child,

You were caught up in a moment of excitement because you were disappointed that you had to leave without the item for which you were searching. Your soul knew you had to connect with the statue so that you could progress further into your spiritual journey. It was a linking process once again in your real world. When you were flying home only then did you realize that the only part of the statue you saw was the hand and arm. At the time you didn't realize that it was a vision. That is why you called your sister and aunt to find out the location of the statue in the church. It was then that you realized you could not have seen the statue from where you were standing. This was a special gift to you my child. This vision was beckoning for you to come follow me. I knew this was the right place to give you this vision because of the memories that were linked with this church. This is the church where you made your first Holy Communion and now once again you were coming to communion with me your Lord and Savior as you progressed and were moving forward with me into your spiritual journey. I was calling you to come follow me, my child.

July 16, 2008

PRAYER:

My Dear Lord;

Do churches play an important part of one's spiritual journey?

ANSWER:

My child;

For some people yes, because it can link them with their past. For you my child, it was because you did not understand what was happening to you. For the devil was fighting with you in the real world. He wanted you to think you were losing your mind. In reality you were entering the spiritual realm. You were beginning a new lifestyle with me, your Lord and Savior. I picked this church for many reasons. The foundation of your beliefs began here and it gave you a sense of security. My child do you remember the very large window on the second story of the church?

The stained glass window has a picture of ivy. I was showing you that this is a message for you my child. The vine represents me and without me you can do nothing. There was a special nun that lived at the convent next door to the church. She was very special in the eyes of God. She had been a convert herself and reached out to everyone no matter what his or her faith was. She loved to play hymns on the organs and sing. Do you remember how she played the very old pump organs where she pushed the pedals with her feet? That organ was there when you started first grade. I was showing you two kinds of organs. It was the beginning of many examples that I have shown you over the years. The term I used was same but different. I was teaching you to keep your focus on the real world and the spiritual world at the same time. It was a constant reminder everyday that you were walking in two worlds, just as the statue was from your real world, but the vision came from the spiritual realm. Both were taking place at the same time. I was teaching you how to walk in the real world and still be able to function as a spiritually led person. Many people can gather information about spiritual journeys but its more difficult walking in the spirit. There are many distractions from Satan and that is why I gave you meanings to each color and numbers to remember. It was I, your Lord and Savior that taught each member of your spiritual family individually the things they needed to learn. It took sometime but eventually you learned it was a form of spiritual warfare my child.

Spiritual Warfare

July 18, 2008

Prayer:

My Dear Lord;

The words *spiritual warfare* are very frightening to someone just stepping into an unknown world. Can you explain this to me Lord?

Answer:

My child;

It is not as frightening as you think. Do you remember your life before your encounter with me through the Holy Spirit? Many things were happening to you in your everyday life, problems after problems, but you were not aware that these attacks were from Satan. You were not aware of all the negative feedbacks that were constantly being played in your mind, which gave you a negative attitude in your life. There are many people in this world going through this. It is unbelievable just how Satan can creep into your unsuspecting lives. It can come through a small crack into even a strong Christian's foundation. It can come in many ways. In people who are not aware of the presence of God. It comes in many ways unknown to them . . . especially teenagers. It comes through the words of their music. The music can destroy the thought process and lead the soul astray. The words in a song can be played over and over through the unknown conscious mind and through choice could lead them in the wrong direction. Even messages on clothing are another way Satan can probe the mind. Do you remember my child how I showed you a tee shirt of a young African American woman who worked with you? On the back, it had a large picture of a martini glass full of liquor advertising a bar. To her it was just a picture or maybe a free shirt; again, she had freedom of choice to wear this item of clothing. However, to the people around her it can become another story. Temptation of liquor is fed to those around her, especially to people who have recovered from alcohol addictions, or could feed the mind of an alcoholic if one is present. In addition, magazines books, movies, TV films or how others teach you to dress are other ways Satan attacks people especially children. Satan loves to use adults to destroy children, through pornography, and sexual attacks that destroys their childhood and trust of other adults. As they grow older, some become child molesters themselves and destroy more lives. The cycle continues. Most people do not understand where this is coming from. It comes from the root and it can go on for generations if not stopped by choice. Satan tempts even people who are Christians through many ways but because of their level or state of understanding can fall to satanic ways, but the choice is always theirs to make.

Many Christians fall into this category of sin. But after the realization of what is happening they repent and ask for forgiveness and come back to me your Lord and Savior. Many use this as a tool of experience of the hell they walked through and are able to reach out to others who are unaware of how Satan comes against them. Many books and movies tell about how God had turned their life around, my child.

July 20, 2008

PRAYER:

My Dear Lord;

I never realized how the attacks of Satan surrounded us in our daily lives. Many of the ways are so hidden. I do not think people are fully aware that it is Satan at work in their lives.

ANSWER:

My child;

This is very true. The underhanded works of Satan is everywhere you turn. My child do you remember how at the beginning of your journey when you went back to Wisconsin to spend time with a very close friend, which you both have the same first name.

REPLY:

"Yes Lord."

ANSWER:

Do you remember how the two of you ventured off to a special church in that area to pray? It was called Holy Hill. This is a place where many people from all over the world go on pilgrimages. This church sits on a small hill and can be seen for miles. My child, there are many reasons why I took you there on your journey with me, your Lord and Savior. First you observed the main alter. There is a picture in the center of the Father,

Son and Holy Spirit. Off to each side is a picture of people at the time you didn't know who they were. Later you learned it was a picture of a woman named St. Teresa of Avila and the other picture was of St. John of the Cross; he was a monk.

Both of these people were extremely close to me your Lord and Savior. St John was the mentor to St. Teresa. Off to the side of this building is a small chapel where there is a large statue of Mary with her eyes looking downward. Her focus is on the small child standing near her. This statue represents how earthly people are to keep their eyes on me. At this cathedral there is a group of men who are Catholic monks. They belong to an order of Carmelite monks. They dress in long brown robes with a white rope around them and they wear sandals. These men have joined this Order for many various reasons. Some of these men are close to God and some not. They also are at different levels or stages of their spiritual growth. Many of them came to God as very young men. Some have chosen a newer lifestyle and some prefer the lifestyle of monks from generations ago. Their walk with God is no different from regular people because temptation is everywhere on the earth. Do you remember the bookstore there?

REPLY:

"Yes my Lord."

ANSWER:

It is full of items the people can purchase to help accommodate the religious walk with me. Still people do not realize that I am everywhere they go.

I see everything they do. I know their every thought. That is why I guided you to this cathedral, to meet with "Little Monk" who became your spiritual director. When you were in the side chapel praying, I also guided a Hispanic woman there. It was there that the two of you shared information about the visions you were seeing of my mother Mary. Remember how she said her name was Maria. I was establishing a pattern for you to follow. Many people who come leave behind crutches and canes for miracles that happen there my child.

LINKING AND SPEAKING IN TONGUES

July 27, 2008

PRAYER:

My Dear Lord;

I find it amazing looking back that there was a pattern to the things I was going through at that time. Do other people notice these patterns in their lives?

ANSWER:

My child;

Not everyone is called to a spiritual journey. Many people seek out spiritual journeys on their own, but at a different level or stage of learning. You my child were called by Me your Lord and Savior for many various reasons. When you were a child, you went through many spiritual attacks but did not realize what was happening to you. Because of your lifestyle then you were able to relate to the poor now. As you grew up your living conditions improved considerably, but your past remains in your memories. It is easy for you to remember what it was like not to have indoor conveniences, like running water and an inside toilet. You lived in a four-room house at one time. So it is easy to relate to the poor. There are many people who can't relate to those who are hungry and live in poor conditions because they have always been blessed in many ways.

I have called you forward to help those in need. Because I know you have a soft heart for touching those who need help. I have blessed you in many ways for a purpose, so that you can share what you have with others. I also called you forward because of your devoted prayer life since you were a child. I also wanted to teach you that Satan can attack in many ways unknown to man. That is why I have become your teacher and your comforter. Through the Holy Spirit, you have been able to be on a journey and observe many things you were not aware of before. A veil has been lifted so that you can touch others around you. A linking process is taking place. When you were learning about colors and how they represented a meaning so that your mind could focus on the spiritual journeys path. The same as the numbers, I taught you my child. This became your spiritual warfare shield or armor. As I guided you to other people on your path, they also learned through the Holy Spirit the same techniques you were learning so that you could have a spiritual family. Your prayer life increased because in faith you grew to be a spiritual warrior. This took great courage in my eyes for you to step out of your box and move forward in your real life and spiritual as well. There have been many blessings given to others because of your choice to come follow me. Many people are not comfortable living this kind of lifestyle because of the attacks of Satan. Yes my child, the attacks can be hard but I do carry you through these attacks mentally and physically. Satan wants people to be discouraged, depressed and angry because during this time in their lives the focus is taken away from me your Lord and Savior. It is during these times that many people break and begin to encounter an experience of finding God in their life. On the battlefield of life one must choose which lifestyle they want. As people grow close to me they learn through experiences of their own how to link to another person going through similar problems. They are able to keep the chain from breaking. People are not aware that it is a fight between good and evil.

In your real world people see this as a form of survival but this is not true. Satan is out to destroy the soul of each person, no matter what tactics he can use. That is why people can come up against you my child.

Sometimes people can become a living vessel for Satan to discourage your from following me, your Lord and Savior. Satan likes to use the people closest to you, ones you love and trust. Sometimes you have to look past the person and sort out the actions that are taking place. You are on a battlefield in your real world and in your mind; your heart and mind are connected. As you feel in your heart so does the mind think and follows. There are many times when people will hate someone but when they learn the reason why someone reacted in a way unknown to them they eventually forgive that person and a close relationship develops again. Sometimes this does not happen because some people have a hard heart. You see my child spiritual warfare is easy if the Holy Spirit leads you.

Do you remember when you were guided to a healing service by your sister? I, your Lord and Savior, again led you unknowingly. You took some close friends and some spiritual family members to this church. There a Catholic priest held the service. Do you remember when he said, we will now pray in tongues and you had no idea what he was saying or what was happening. Most of the people began to speak in a different language you never heard of before. As I watched you I felt sorrow for you because you did not understand what was happening to you. You observed the man that was with you as he began to speak in tongues. I remember you grabbing him by the shirt collar and shaking him. You asked, "What are you doing?" Then you sat down, put your hands over your face and wept. You had reached a breaking point where you were thinking that you had died and went somewhere else but that the people looked the same. Then you stood up and you heard me say, "Nancy, just hum." Then you began to speak in another language unknown to you. You received the Gift of Tongues my child.

July 29, 2008

PRAYER:

My Dear Lord;

I remember that night when I first heard the praying in tongues. Now when I think back to that night I feel very embarrassed by my reactions Lord. Please forgive me.

Answer:

My child;

I realize that you were in a state of confusion. Many things were happening to you during this time. Your body was changing during this time and you thought you were going through menopause. Also your youngest child had just left home two weeks before and then you thought that you were having a mental breakdown. But this is not true my child. You had lived your life according to your choices in life, but now while you were praying because you wanted help with another child you felt hopeless with the circumstances. That is when I heard your plea for help. It was then that your spiritual journey with me, your Lord and Savior, began. You never heard about spiritual journeys. I was teaching you as you progressed on your walk with me.

There are many people who never experienced a rebirth through the Holy Spirit, which is why people never share stories of their walk with God. Many people are ashamed or keep it hidden from others that they see visions or hear voices speaking to them. In the real world they are categorized as being crazy or ill, but as I have taught you there are stepping stones when one is on a spiritual journey. It doesn't all come at one time, seeing visions, hearing voices and praying with a new prayer language is only a small part of a spiritual journey. A rebirth had taken place and a whole new life with Christ began with you my child. You had a very difficult beginning with your spiritual journey because Satan wanted your soul that is why you had to fight him in your mind and real world. Do you remember the day you did not want to go to work because the voice you were hearing was telling you that you were going to die on the way? I watched you cry as you drove your car and when you got to the stop sign you looked up into your rear view mirror and saw a black Z28 vehicle speeding up behind you but it swerved just in time from hitting you. I heard you scream a prayer for the man who drove through the intersection at a fast speed. All the lanes were full. My child, do you remember how you heard dead silence until he passed through the intersection. Then as if someone turned on a switch, you could hear the birds singing and horns blowing as he passed through. Yes my child, I was showing you that I can be in control of the things that happen. I was sparing your life for a reason my child.

⁓

July 30, 2008

PRAYER:

My Dear Lord;

Yes Lord, I remember that scenario I went through. My daughter went through a similar accident a couple of years before. The thought that ran through my mind was her car was totaled and she did not die so it was repeating the story and this time I would die.

ANSWER:

No my child;

It was not your time to die. It was a satanic attack; the devil was trying to scare you. He wanted you to fail on your spiritual journey by feeding you those thoughts so you would not go to work. In your real world, this is known as a panic attack, but remember how frustrated you were when your husband told you just to go . . . nothing's going to happen to you. That was a message from me my child. My blood covered you. Yes, I was teaching you that I am in control. Remember the car swerved around you. I did not allow you to hear sound for a time. Everything happens for a reason my child.

WEAPONS OF WARFARE

August 1, 2008

PRAYER:

My Dear Lord;

There were many things you were teaching me at that time Lord, but why did you want me to experience the things that I couldn't understand or explain to others?

ANSWER:

My child;

I allowed these events to take place in your life for many reasons. If you had heard about spiritual warfare from other people, you would not have understood what they were telling you. You needed to come head-to-head with Satan in order to understand what others experience in their lives. You had walked the path so that you had a full understanding of what it is like to fight Satan. My child do you remember when I told you I wanted you to attend another church service that was different from the denomination you were raised in. You were full of fear and you had to go alone. I wanted you to meet others that were like you. There was a purpose for you to see and observe other people in this little church. I wanted you to meet the visiting pastor Coleman and his wife Mary at Faith Chapel.

They were both speaking on "Weapons of Our Warfare." I was linking you with these people so you could learn more on spiritual warfare. I was blending your spiritual side of life with the real world and did you notice that her name was Mary, my child?

✑

September 28, 2008

PRAYER:

My Dear Lord;

I remember attending that service. I had never heard of weapons of warfare before. Lord, are these weapons important to Christians?

ANSWER:

Yes, my child;

There are many forms of spiritual warfare. Praise and worship are very important because during this time people begin to feel the presence of God. It was during this service that you heard that God was sending a revival to this land and that the people would be called warriors in the army of God. It was there that you learned that the most powerful tool of warfare is prayer itself. I wanted you to learn that praying in your spiritual language was the greatest form of warfare for you. This is a gift from God.

There are many forms of prayer, from the simplest whisper of my name, Jesus to the many ways that are taught in the Bible.

Satan wants you to think that there are boundaries but this is not true. When two or more are gathered together in my name, I will be in your midst. Through prayer, bondages can be broken. Remember the word of God is our sword. Spiritual warfare is a mighty tool against Satan. These lessons are not always taught in seminaries. As each person receives the gift of the Holy Spirit, each is led by the Spirit individually according to their spiritual walk with the Lord. As the Holy Spirit begins to work in your life, you begin to have to make choices. The spirit will lead you in new directions rather than the old way you use to live and a total transformation can take place. Some people refer to our old ways as living in the flesh. Many people are not able to follow the Holy Spirit because they have to change their old ways of thinking. The temptations from Satan are strong because he wants you to fall away from listening to the Holy Spirit. He is out to destroy your path with me, your Lord and Savior. I am always there to help guide you in your decisions to walk with me. Many times people are not strong enough to keep their eyes on me and they fall away. Some call this backsliding or drifting. That is why it is so important to learn about spiritual warfare, my child.

October 13, 2008

PRAYER:

My Dear Lord;

What can you tell me about praying in tongues?

Many people are fearful of people who pray in tongues, even me, at the beginning of my spiritual journey. I did not understand what was happening.

ANSWER:

My child;

This is something you do not have to fear. Speaking in tongues is a special gift from God. In the Bible, there is a story of how the people received the gift of tongues. Not everyone is called to this gift. Your prayer language, as some people refer to this is a communication between your soul and God; it's a language that the devil cannot interrupt. It is a prayer whispered to me, your Lord and Savior, which you do not understand.

My child, do you remember on September 28, 2008, a Sunday when a visiting pastor came to your church? His name was Pastor Rudy. As he walked down the aisle, he stopped and looked at you and said that you are a woman of God.

"Give me your hand," he said.

He held your hand in the air and prayed this prayer.

"Lord, this woman has been waiting for a long time for her harvest to come."

Pastor Rudy knew you were called beginning at the age of eight. I sent this pastor to intercede on your behalf because you were afraid to ask for your harvest even after Pastor Joel told you to ask for your harvest. You have planted many seeds to help others, but you were fearful of the attacks of Satan. I sent Pastor Rudy for this purpose to teach you not to be afraid and to let you know that I am in control!

Do you remember when Pastor Rudy had an alter call and hugged you and then pressed his cheek against the side of your face? The thought came to your mind that this felt the same as when you pray. How you feel my presence next to you.

REPLY:

"Yes Lord."

ANSWER:

Then do you remember how the two of you began to pray in tongues together.

REPLY:

"Yes Lord, I do remember."

ANSWER:

Then all of a sudden you began to pray in English, but it was not a prayer that you were thinking in your mind. In fact, you were listening to yourself speak, and you were hearing your own voice. Your soul was praying and thanking the Heavenly Father for sending this man to your church as this was an answer to your prayer. I smiled when you said this because it was your soul that had made the request and not you my child. As you were listening to your voice speaking, you asked me through your thoughts "What prayer?" I replied when you prayed in tongues. You continued your prayer asking that he may bless thousands of people and at the conclusion of your prayer, Pastor Rudy walked away but then he stopped and returned to you, smiled at you, and said, "Thank you mighty warrior." That was a message from me your Lord and Savior. I gave you a very special gift that day on the ninth month, the twenty-eighth day of two thousand and eight, my child.

October 15, 2008

PRAYER:

My Dear Lord;

Thank you for bringing Pastor Rudy into my life and letting him be a human vessel for you. Were there other lessons there for me and others to learn?

ANSWER:

Yes, my child;

Do you remember the sermon he spoke that day? It was mainly on the importance of my mother, Mary. It was her choice to be open to the Holy Spirit. She became an example for people to follow. It was her willingness to say yes. My child, this is so important to be open to the Holy Spirit so that you can receive direct instruction on how to follow your path on your spiritual journey with me, your Lord and Savior. I was teaching you that I can combine your real world with the supernatural world. I can use pastors to give direct messages to groups and sometimes to individuals. Did you also notice that I brought Pastor Rudy back on the tenth month, the fifth day, of two thousand and eight my child?

⌒∦⌒

November 1, 2008

PRAYER:

My Dear Lord;

I do not fully understand how my real world and the supernatural world can combine themselves, but I do know you are present and I know you are working in my life. I can see a pattern of events taking place and I realize that I have no control over what is taking place. Lord are you taking me in a special direction and may I ask "why?"

ANSWER:

My child;

You ask so many important questions and all at one time. Your real world and supernatural world are blending for a very specific reason; through the Holy Spirit my work is being accomplished. I cannot tell you what is happening behind the scenes at this time, but in the future, it will be revealed to you my child.

I have placed you and Pastor Rudy together for a very important reason. I have assigned you as his personal prayer warrior. This is a new level for you my child. During your everyday routines at the factory or at your home it is I your Lord and Savior who brings his name or face to your mind so that you can pray for him. During this time of intercession, you can be in constant prayer for him. You may pray in your natural or prayer language for your soul understands the will of my Father, my child.

⌒∦⌒

November 2, 2008

PRAYER:

My Dear Lord;

When Pastor Rudy prayed for my harvest to come in is that why I fell into another scenario that involved Dr. Rodney Howard-Browne's Revival that came to the city of Phoenix?

ANSWER:

Yes, my child;

This was a very important part of your spiritual journey. Do you remember many years ago, in 1994, when I told you to turn on the TV and that is when you saw Rodney for the first time?

This is how I taught you about resting in the spirit and you witnessed holy laughter. Some people call this "drunk in the Spirit." There were many times when you fell to the floor and could not move a finger. You were experiencing resting in the spirit and had no idea what was happening to you at the time. I brought Rodney to Phoenix because he is praying for a revival that is coming into the United States. As he said, the Lord told him, that the revival will hit the Latino communities. Do you see my presence my child?

REPLY:

"Yes, Lord I do."

ANSWER:

Did you notice that there were five churches that opened their doors to his ministries my child?

REPLY:

"Yes Lord, I did."

ANSWER:

Remember how I taught you how to watch for the number five? The first church I sent you to was on 19th Avenue. I was showing you that 1 and 9 is 10. It is a high five between you and I. Did you also notice before the service started you could feel the flow of the Holy Spirit entering the room?

REPLY:

"Yes Lord, it was amazing."

ANSWER:

Do you remember how Rodney said that it's time to bring in the "harvest?"

REPLY:

"Yes, Lord, I will always remember what he said."

ANSWER:

Then I sent you to another church on 27th Avenue. The other number I told you to watch for was number 9. So 2 and 7 equals 9. Yes, my child you are on a very special spiritual journey with me your Lord and Savior. Also the revival will take place mainly in the Hispanic communities that is why I have placed you mainly with these people in your walk with me. I want you to observe the works of the Holy Spirit my child.

HARVEST OF SOULS

November 9, 2008

PRAYER:

My Dear Lord;

I feel over whelmed as I write to you today Lord, because you are showing me the harvest of souls. I cry as I write to you this morning, for I can see your work in action. Last night I was invited to attend a Christian concert. The guest was Eddie James and the Praise Band. What I saw really touched my soul Jesus. Did I see what you sent me there to observe?

ANSWER:

Yes, my child;

The reason you are crying is because your soul is feeling the hurt of the souls in the harvest my child. There were many things there that I wanted you to see and hear. First of all this event took place on 91st Avenue; 9 and 1 equals 10 (our high five) my child.

Through your friend, Paul, it was I that arranged for you to have a center front seat. I did not want you to miss a single thing. Eddie James is a man who is in my heart, a true man of God. Because of his own life, he is able to minister to young men and women who suffer the attacks of Satan. He spoke on how I am boxed in, in organized churches or religious rituals. This is true my child, for I am in your everyday life, minute by minute, when you are away from church buildings and pastors. For very few people openly speak how Satan attacks in our everyday life.

Do you remember the drama team as they performed a story of a young woman who was close to me your Lord and Savior, but then the real world events began to take place in her life? A young man gets her attentions then he rejects her. Then she is drawn to money then it is taken away. Then someone introduces her to liquor, from there she turns to prostitution then as her final step, she tries to commit suicide, but at the last minute, she cries out to the Lord. I step in and save her. These are only a few ways Satan can attack my child. For Satan attacks the young and the old alike. As some of the young people gave their stories on how broken their lives were did you notice that some were sons of pastors?

REPLY:

"Yes Lord, I did."

ANSWER:

The other thing I wanted you to see was that there were some young men there who were wearing rosaries around their necks. Have you noticed, my child, the closer you draw to me the more attacks of Satan are heavily against you or your loved ones. Satan wants to destroy your lives because you are living vessels for me my child. Many people are not aware of the attacks children go through on a daily basis. It is not openly spoken about and is hidden as if it does not exist and as the child grows older the attacks become more severe as time moves on until they reach a point of destruction. Many people do not recognize the attacks and then it is passed on to the next generation. This is a silent killer of souls, my child.

November 20, 2008

PRAYER:

My Dear Lord;

Many events seem to be taking place in my life at a very fast pace. Lord is there a special reason why this is happening to me?

ANSWER:

Yes, my child;

One event after another is taking place. I want you to be fully aware of my presence at this time for many reasons. I want you to put your full trust in me. As you see, it was I who brought Rabito's concert to your church. His testimony touched many hearts there. My child did you feel the presence of the Almighty God?

REPLY:

"Yes, Lord I did."

ANSWER:

This church was located at 27ᵗʰ Avenue and Thomas. Once again, 2 and 7 equals 9. At the beginning of your spiritual journey, do you remember how your husband use to call you the 'doubting Saint Thomas'?

REPLY:

"Yes, my Lord, I remember but Father, I have seen so many times your interaction in my life that I know its not possible for a human to lay out those plans for my life continuously year after year, event after event because the people involved do not even understand the number system you have taught me. Or even the phrase 'Nancy, the doubting St. Thomas.'

ANSWER:

This is correct my child, this is something I, your Lord and Savior taught you on your spiritual path with me. I wanted to help you keep your awareness of me with you on your daily walk with me.

Many people are in turmoil right now not knowing which way to turn. Between family problems and the economy, my children are suffering. The Bible writes how my children suffer from lack of knowledge. Yet if people would read the Bible there are many, many passages on how people can lean on me your Lord and Savior. For through the Holy Spirit, I can direct your path on a daily basis, but you must believe in me give me your full trust, your love, your attention and most of all the thing I desire the most, a personal relationship with me your Heavenly Father my child. Through me, I am able to protect you against the attacks of Satan. I can help you to make decisions that will keep your life from falling apart. Remember my child; you always have the freedom of choice in every matter that comes your way. I have allowed you to walk the spiritual path with me; your Lord and Savior for a special reason my child. Yes, for when you were a little girl you were very close to my mother Mary and through your relationship with her, I allowed that path to take place. Do you remember the statue of Mary standing on top of a globe and beneath her feet is a snake?

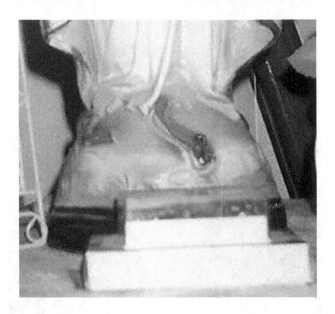

REPLY:

"Yes Lord I do."

ANSWER:

When you were little, you once asked a nun why Mary is standing on top of a snake. She told you at the end of time Mary will crush out Satan, but you didn't understand what she was telling you my child because it was not your time but the seed was planted in your brain. Your desire at a very young age was to be a nun and teacher. This plan never occurred. I closed the doors for I had other plans for you my child. After your last child left home, it was I your Lord and Savior who called you into a new life of spiritually walking with me. Do you remember when I told you that you made all the choices for your life and of raising the children, I gave you that, now your life belongs to me. This is why the devil tried so hard at the beginning to destroy your life in the real world and your spiritual side. I was at your side the entire time while you were battling Satan. I allowed you to go through these scenarios for a reason so that you could have experiences and live through them so that you could teach firsthand about the experiences of your walk with me, your Lord and Savior. This is why I told you that many barriers and old beliefs needed to be broken. Only through this process would you become a powerful prayer warrior just like Pastor Rudy. Through the stories you share with others, doors will open for those who need real world guidance on their spiritual journeys. My child it was I, your heavenly Father that was there all the time walking with you. Just like the stories that are handed down through the generations of the people in the Bible. My child I wanted you to be a teacher for many because people are not open to sharing what is happening to them in their spiritual life. Many like you do not understand what is happening to them. Many people feel as if they are having mental breakdowns. Many are being given labels because they hear voices speaking to them and people do not understand that Satan speaks to you also. It is a battleground between good and evil. They need to learn how to discern and choose a loving relationship with me, your Heavenly Father through my advocate the Holy Spirit. Together, you can learn to be strong and like a puzzle piece fit together and become strong links with one another my child. This is why I gave you two spiritual families. As their faith grew I removed them from you, so they could move on and touch others around them. You have gathered a lot of information over the years walking with me my child.

Through the stories, you will be able to strengthen my people who will be beginning a spiritual journey of their own. Many people are not aware of the Holy Spirit, or like you did at the beginning did not read the Bible. Nor do they ever really learn the importance of the Holy Spirit.

For after my son died on the cross, I sent the Holy Spirit into your world to help direct your path to me your loving Father, but remember you always have a freedom of choice in every matter. Remember I sent my son into the world to become a human living vessel just like you. The Bible leaves a trail of wonderful stories about visions, people hearing from God and how some choose to follow and some did not. Some suffered because they did not listen and there were times when I walked away and left people to struggle on their own. It is a choice to have a relationship with me your Lord and Savior. You are a new spring time to others as you try to open doors into the spiritual life of each person you meet as you have with me your Lord and Savior.

My child, do you remember at one time you thought a space creature was talking to you through your thoughts and you thought the vision of a cookbook was how you were going to be destroyed? Do you remember the fear you felt at that time? I was in control. I sent someone to you at that time and he told you to mentally turn the book around and to your surprise you saw my Son hanging on a cross. The heading read, "How to Serve Man." My child, I was with you all the time. It is very important for you to trust and believe in me your Lord and Savior, my child.

WALK WITH ME

December 28, 2008

PRAYER:

My Dear Lord;

I can hardly believe I have finished writing my journal in one year's time and even after the second writing, I felt as if I were struggling for questions to ask you for you are the Lord of our universe. I did not know what direction this journal was going in. I want to thank you Lord for all the beautiful questions and answers you have given me. With high hopes, it is my greatest desire to help others who are on their spiritual journey. This has been a challenging experience for me, but through faith and a great love for you I was able to pull both of my feet into the spiritual realm and I learned to fight to keep my eyes focused on you my Lord and Savior.

ANSWER:

My Dear Child;

You underwent a test of faith not knowing what was happening to you. Many years ago, Pope John XXIII called together the Second Vatican Council and prayed for a new Pentecost in our days, but you were not aware of people who were spiritually led. You had no clue. That is why you battled Satan head on and through this, you became a very strong Spiritual Warrior. Your strong faith in me, your Lord and Savior carried you through many horrifying scenarios. Your love for me never failed. In fact, your love grew stronger and stronger as time went on. However, as for hope there seems to be very little at this time because you do not know the direction you should go in.

My child put your life into my hands, as you have done before. Walk with me. I know you are upset because I have separated you from your spiritual family members but it was done for a reason my child. My love for you grows every day. You have been faithful to me as you follow my directions through the Holy Spirit. Many years ago, you were escorted out of a prayer group for being too spiritual. Do you remember how you opened your mouth and out came, "I want unity among my people?"

REPLY:

"Yes Lord, I remember." I was so frightened by this experience because my brain and mouth were not working together. I just listened to my own voice speak on its own.

ANSWER:

It was I your Lord and Savior who put those words there not you. My hope and desire for you my child is to continue your Spiritual Journey with me. I am offering you a spiritual gift. Come follow me. You are a light that exposes darkness. You make people aware of their thoughts and with whom they speak. You are links to one another. You are living the stories in the Bible. Keep your eyes on me and come follow me my child.

My Little Dancer.

To contact the author with questions or for speaking engagements, please write to:

Nancy Wiltgen
P.O. Box 46240
Phoenix, AZ 85063